MATH Word Problems Made Easy

Grade 2

by Bob Krech

NEW YORK • TORONTO • LONDON • AUCKLAND • SYDNEY
MEXICO CITY • NEW DELHI • HONG KONG • BUENOS AIRES

Teaching *Resources*

Dedication

To Mr. Ron Rosen, super 7th-grade math teacher, wherever you are!

Acknowledgements

Many thanks to Maryann McMahon-Nester
for her creative problem contributions

Cover design by Maria Lilja
Interior design by Holly Grundon
Interior illustrations by Mike Moran

ISBN 0-439-52970-0
Copyright © 2005 by Bob Krech
All rights reserved.
Printed in the U.S.A.

2 3 4 5 6 7 8 9 10   40   12 11 10 09 08 07 06 05

CONTENTS

INTRODUCTION

Problem solving is the first of the process standards listed in the *Principles and Standards for School Mathematics* (NCTM, 2000). Being selected as number one is not surprising in view of this accompanying statement from the National Council of Teachers of Mathematics (NCTM): *"Problem solving should be the central focus of all mathematics instruction and an integral part of all mathematical activity."* In other words, in mathematics, problem solving is what it's all about.

When learning to read, we learn to recognize the letters of the alphabet, we practice letter–sound relationships, and we learn punctuation; it's all about eventually being able to read text. A similar situation exists in math. We learn how to recognize and write numerals, decipher symbols, determine numerical order, and work with operations like addition and subtraction. But it's all about what we can do with these skills—applying what we know to solve problems in daily life!

Math Word Problems Made Easy: Grade 2 is designed to help you help your students learn more about and increase their problem-solving abilities, and thus their personal math power. This book is divided into three main sections to help you:

The Fantastic Five-Step Process

The first section describes a simple five-step problem-solving process and introductory lesson you can share with your students. This process can be used with every math word problem they might encounter. This is a valuable concept to introduce at the beginning of the year and practice with students so that they will have an approach they can rely on as they encounter various types of problems.

The Super Seven Strategies

In this section, we look at the various types of problems students might encounter and the super seven strategies for approaching them. We discuss each strategy and then provide five sample problems suitable for solving with that strategy. This gives students an opportunity to practice the strategy in a context of math content appropriate to their grade level. You may want to introduce a new strategy every week or so. This way, by the end of the second month of school, students are familiar with all of the basic strategies and have had practice with them.

The Happy Hundred Word Problems

The third section is a collection of 100 math word problems focused on math concepts specific to second grade. The problems are written so students will find them fun and interesting (and maybe a little silly). No doubt about it, funny problems focus students' attention. It is much more fun and motivating for students to read about Pierre the Talking Circus Dog as he shops for a hairbrush than it is to consider when the legendary two trains will pass each other.

The problems are arranged by mathematical standard; there are sections of problems for Number and Operations, Measurement, Data Analysis and Probability, and Geometry. The individual problems are printed two to a page with a line dividing them, leaving plenty of work space for students to show their thinking. These problems can be used to introduce a concept, practice application of it, or as an end point to check for understanding.

Learning a consistent problem-solving process approach, becoming familiar with and practicing effective problem-solving strategies, and applying these ideas in word-problem contexts help students become more effective problem solvers and mathematicians. And with *Math Word Problems Made Easy: Grade 2*, they can have fun while doing it!

The Fantastic Five-Step Process

What do you do when you first encounter a math word problem? This is what we need to help students deal with. We need to help them develop a process that they can use effectively to solve any type of math word problem.

Word problems often intimidate students because there may be a lot of information; the important facts are embedded in text; and, unlike a regular equation, it is not always clear exactly what you are supposed to do. No matter what type of problem students encounter, these five steps will help them through it. Learning and using the five steps will help students *organize* their interpretation and thinking about the problem. This is the key to good problem solving—organizing for action.

The best way to help students understand the process is to demonstrate using it as you work through a problem on the board or overhead. Make a copy of the graphic organizer on page 7. You can blow this up into a poster or provide each student with his or her own copy to refer back to as you bring students through this introductory lesson.

The Fantastic Five-Step Process

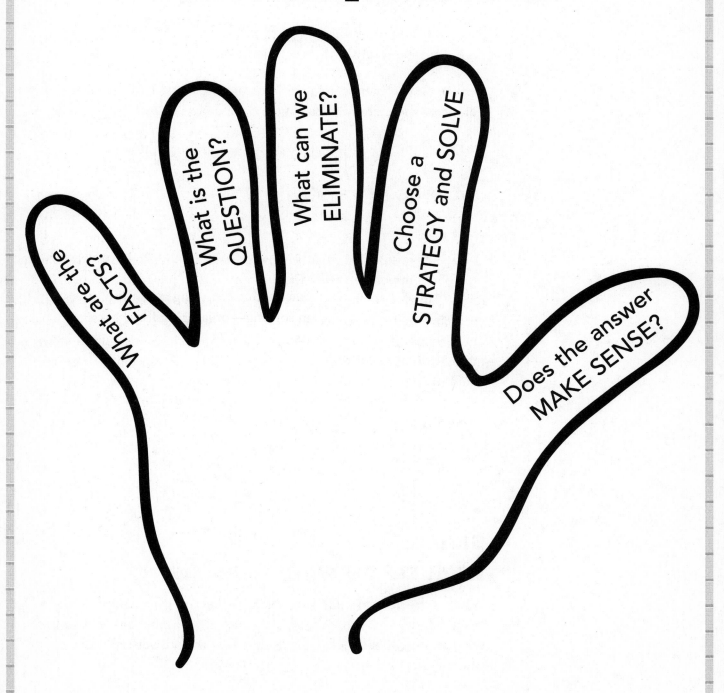

What are the FACTS?

What is the QUESTION?

What can we ELIMINATE?

Choose a STRATEGY and SOLVE

Does the answer MAKE SENSE?

Step 1:
What Do We Know?

Begin by writing this problem on the board or overhead.

> Jock had 6 lima bean-flavored gumdrops in his candy jar. His brother Jack had 8. His sister, Jinx, had 12. Jinx said Jack had more than Jock. Is she right? If so, how many more?

Read the problem carefully. What are the facts? Have students volunteer these orally. Write them on the board.

> Jock had 6 gumdrops.
> Jack had 8 gumdrops.
> Jinx had 12 gumdrops.

Encourage students to write down the facts. This will help them focus on what is important while looking for ways to put it in a more accessible form. Can we arrange the facts in a way that will help us understand the problem situation? For instance, maybe it would be good to draw what we know, or put it in a list, or make a table. Sometimes it's helpful to arrange numbers from lower to higher or higher to lower, especially if we are asked to compare. Are we being asked to compare? Yes!

> Jinx – 12
> Jack – 8
> Jock – 6

Step 2:
What Do We Want to Know?

What is the question in the problem? What are we trying to find out? It is a good idea to have students state the question and also determine how the answer will be labeled. For example, if the answer is 7, then it's 7 what? 7 cats? 7 coins?

We want to know two things:
1. Was Jinx right when she said Jack had more gumdrops than Jock?
2. How many more gumdrops does Jack have than Jock?

Step 3:
What Can We Eliminate?

Once we know what we are trying to find out, we can decide what is unimportant. We may need all the information, but often there is extra information that can be put aside to help focus on the facts.

We can eliminate the fact that Jinx had 12 gumdrops. It's not needed to answer the question. We're left with

Jack — 8
Jock — 6

By comparing the numbers, we can answer the first part of the question now. Jinx was right. Jack has more.

Step 4:
Choose a Strategy or Action and Solve

Is there an action in the story (for example, is something being "taken away" or is something being "shared") that will help us decide on an operation or a way to solve the problem?

Since we have to compare something we have to find the **difference**. Usually the best way is to subtract or add up. This is the action we need to do.

$$\begin{array}{r} 8 \\ -6 \\ \hline 2 \end{array}$$

So Jack had 2 more gumdrops than Jock.

Step 5:
Does Our Answer Make Sense?

Reread the problem. Look at the answer. Is it reasonable? Is it a sensible answer given what we know?

It makes sense. For one, 2 is a lower number than the higher number we started with. If it was higher, that would be a problem because the difference between two whole positive numbers cannot be higher than the highest number.

Try a number of different word problems using this "talk through" format with students. You can use sample problems from throughout the book. You might invite students to try the problem themselves first and then debrief step-by-step together, sharing solutions along with you to see if all steps were considered and solutions are, in fact, correct. Practicing the process in this way helps make it part of a student's way of thinking mathematically.

The Super Seven Strategies

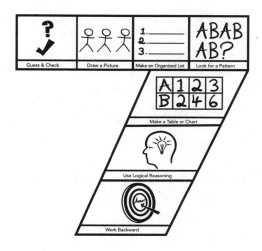

? ✓	👤👤👤	1. ___ 2. ___ 3. ___	ABAB AB?
Guess & Check	Draw a Picture	Make an Organized List	Look for a Pattern

A	1	2	3
B	2	4	6

Make a Table or Chart

Use Logical Reasoning

Work Backward

While we should encourage the use of the Five-Step Process to approach any problem, Step 4 (Choose a Strategy or Action and Solve) includes a wide range of choices. Some common strategies that are helpful to teach and practice are listed on the next few pages with sample problems. Students should have experience with all of the strategies. The more practice they have, the easier it will be for them to choose a strategy that fits the problem and helps deliver an answer.

Tip

As students learn about and practice using these strategies to solve problems, ask them to create their own problems. You can list the math concepts you want in the problems (such as addition or money) and even the strategy that must be used to solve it. Students use these parameters to create their own problems, which they can share and try out with one another. As students begin to play with these elements, their knowledge of how problems work grows, as does their confidence when encountering new problems.

STRATEGY 1:
Guess & Check

GUESS & CHECK

"**G**uess and Check" means if you're not sure what to do, begin with a reasonable guess to get you started. Look for key words and phrases, like "all together" or "more than," that may help move you in the right direction in choosing an operation. Students should be urged to look at the numbers in the problem and try to apply their estimation skills. This is the key to making a "reasonable" guess. Even just this first step is worth practicing. Then when a first attempted answer is arrived at, consider whether the answer is reasonable, too high, or too low. This is the "Check" part of Guess and Check.

After considering the answer, decide if you need to revise and how. Would a higher answer make sense? A lower answer? A good way to share this strategy with your class is to try one of the following problems on the board and think aloud with them through the steps. Talk out loud as you decide on your first attempt. Explain why you chose that number or numbers. Then talk to them about how you are examining the number to determine if it is reasonable. Talk about how you are adjusting your initial attempt and why.

Answers

1. Jenny is 56 inches tall. Jeanie is 52 inches tall.

2. 3 quarters, 1 nickel, and 2 pennies OR 1 half-dollar, 3 dimes, and 2 pennies

3. 3 8-packs of soda and 4 pizzas

4. 5 inches of snow

5. Gooey Garlic Gumdrops, Sneaky's Sneeze Powder, and Rodent Ring Pops

SAMPLE PROBLEMS

1. Jeanie and Jenny are almost identical twins. They look exactly the same except that Jenny is 4 inches taller than Jeanie. If together they measure 9 feet tall, how tall is each girl?

2. Forgetful Frank was always forgetting where he put his lunch money. So on Friday, he put his money in a special place. "82 cents, please," said Mrs. Muncher, the lunch lady. Frank reached into his sock and took out 6 coins that equaled exactly 82¢. What coins did Frank take from his sock?

3. The Burpsie-Cola Company sells their pickle-flavored soda in packs of 8. Piping Hot Pizza cuts their turnip-topped pizza pies into 12 slices. At the end-of-the-year party, each of the 24 children in Miss Alex's Unusual Art class will be served one can of soda and 2 slices of pizza. How many packs of soda and how many pizza pies does Miss Alex need to order?

4. Miss Frosty's second-grade class just learned the famous "Let It Snow" dance and was asked to practice it for homework over the weekend. By Monday, there had been 3 separate snowstorms and a total of 35 inches of snow had fallen! If each snowstorm left twice as much snow as the one before it, how much snow fell in the first storm?

5. Wacky Walter went to Strange-But-Neat Treats to buy treats for his birthday party. He bought 3 different packages and spent $10.65. What did Walter buy?

Gooey Garlic Gumdrops	$2.85
Lizard Tongue Lollipops	$5.10
Sneaky's Sneeze Powder	$4.63
Rodent Ring Pops	$3.17
Brussels Sprout Bubble Gum	$1.89

Draw a Picture

DRAW A PICTURE

Drawing a picture can help answer the question in the first step of the problem-solving process: "What do we know?" Sometimes words do not easily convey the facts. Sometimes they can even confuse. By having students draw what they know, the problem can become clearer, and students can arrange and manipulate the facts more easily and discover relationships more quickly.

When students use drawings or diagrams to help solve problems, remind them that they are not creating artwork. Unnecessary details or coloring should be left out. This is also a good occasion to introduce the idea of using simple symbols to represent elements of a word problem, such as a triangle for trees or a simple stick figure for people.

Answers

1. 6 goals

2. 48 square feet

3. 27 worms

4. 60 cups

5. 22 children: 7 boys and 15 girls

SAMPLE PROBLEMS

1. Superstar soccer player Sylvester Slug scored one goal every 15 minutes during the Slug Soccer World Championship game. If the game lasted $1\frac{1}{2}$ hours, how many goals did Sylvester score?

2. Theodore Q. Bear is tired of spending winter after winter hibernating in his cold cave. He has decided that wall-to-wall carpeting will warm up the place. If his cave measures 8 feet long and 6 feet wide, how much carpet should he order from www.happyhibernatingcarpets.com?

3. Sidney Squigglesworth collects worms. One warm afternoon while walking in the woods, Sidney found more worms for his collection. He placed 3 worms in each pocket. He had 4 pockets in his pants, 2 pockets in his shirt, and 3 in his jacket. How many worms did Sidney add to his collection that day?

4. Roger Fizzle is in charge of running the filling machine at the Frosty Fizz Soda Pop Company. On Tuesday afternoon the filling machine mysteriously stopped filling soda-pop bottles. Roger had to fill the last 15 quart-sized bottles by hand. He used an 8-ounce cup. How many cups did Roger have to pour to fill all of the bottles?

5. Miss Deidre Diagram drew a picture of her classroom's desk arrangement for the substitute, Mr. Patrick Patience. There were 3 groups of 4 desks and 2 groups of 5 desks. One boy sat at each group of 4 and 2 boys sat at each group of 5. How many children are in Miss Diagram's class? How many are boys and how many are girls?

Make an Organized List

1._____

2._____

3._____

_____

MAKE AN ORGANIZED LIST

"**M**ake an Organized List" is strategy that helps us identify and organize what we know. In problems where, for example, combinations must be determined, listing all possible combinations is essential. Compiling a list can help students see if they have considered all possibilities. Lists, as well as drawings, can also help reveal patterns that may exist.

As an introduction to this strategy it may be helpful for students to use or make manipulatives as they create their lists of data. For example, if you ask students to find all the possible combinations of shorts and T-shirts when you have a red T-shirt, a green T-shirt, a white pair of shorts, and a pink pair of shorts, you might have them use colored cubes to represent the clothes, or color and cut out some simple drawings of the clothes. Students can then list each combination of manipulatives.

Answers

1. 15 days

2. 6 different combinations

3. 3 quarters and 2 dimes AND 1 half-dollar, 1 quarter, 1 dime, and 2 nickels

4. 10 tunes

5. 6 different orders

SAMPLE PROBLEMS

1. To get ready for her Alaska cruise, Georgina bought 3 scarves (one striped, one dotted, and one with stars) and 5 colored pairs of socks (blue, orange, yellow, red, and lavender). On each day of the cruise, Georgina wore a different combination of one scarf and one pair of socks. She wore every possible combination once till the end of the cruise. How long was the cruise?

2. Old Weber Wizard created a memory potion to cure forgetfulness, but forgot to write down the potion's ingredients. All he could remember was that he used equal amounts of 2 ingredients. He looked at the 4 bottles on his desk: Elephant Memory, Toad Thoughts, Iguana Ideas, and Walrus Wishes. How many possible combinations are there?

3. On the island of Moola, money grows on trees. Each morning Todd and Tad "pick" their lunch money from the coin tree in their backyard. One Friday, they each picked 5 coins and each had exactly 95¢. However, they did not have the same combination of coins. What two combinations of coins did they pick?

4. The Harmonyville Harmonica Competition is scheduled for noon Saturday at Intune Park. 2 boys and 3 girls are entered in the competition. In round one, each musician must play a short (duet) tune with each of the other musicians. How many tunes will be played in round one?

5. Dorothy is the owner and only employee of the Disappearing Dust cleaning service. At each house, Dorothy dusts, vacuums, does dishes, and clears clutter. To make her job exciting, she changes the order of some jobs at each house. If Dorothy always saves vacuuming for last, how many different orders are possible?

Look for a Pattern

ABAB AB?

LOOK FOR A PATTERN

Using lists and drawing pictures help reveal patterns that may exist within the information a problem supplies. The guiding question for discovering patterns is, "What relationships do you see between the numbers in the problem?" How far apart are they from each other? Do they increase or decrease by certain amounts in certain ways? Asking these questions will often lead to a good solution.

In a problem where we are told that Surelook lived at 222 Beaker Street and that his next-door neighbor on his left lived at 220, we could use a pattern to tell what the address of the person living on his right, two doors down would be (226). Number lines, hundred charts, and calculators can be useful tools in helping students recognize a pattern that may exist in a problem.

Answers

1. 14 grams
2. Saturday
3. 9 inch
4. 10 fried-eel sandwiches
5. 45 force fuel points

SAMPLE PROBLEMS

1. Herman the Hermit Crab has entered the Sand Dune Weight-Lifting Competition. On day #1, he lifts 2 grams. On day #2, he lifts 4 grams. On day #3, he lifts 6 grams. If he continues this pattern, how much weight will he lift in the competition on day #7?

2. Andrew the Aardvark eats only in even numbers. This week he ate 24 ants on Monday, 30 ants on Tuesday, and 36 ants on Wednesday. Following this pattern, on which day will he eat 54 ants?

3. Jolly Jangles Joke Shop sells the best bouncing rubber eyeballs in the business. A 1-inch round eyeball bounces 4 inches. A 3-inch round eyeball bounces 12 inches. A 5-inch round eyeball bounces 20 inches. Rupert needs an eyeball that will bounce exactly 36 inches. What size eyeball should he buy?

4. In November Finicky Frances ate only 3 types of sandwiches. On Nov. 1st she ate peanut butter with marshmallows. On Nov. 2nd she ate fried eel with mustard. On Nov. 3rd she ate spaghetti with mayonnaise. On Nov. 4th she was back to the peanut butter, and on the 5th it was fried eel again. If she continues this pattern, how many fried-eel sandwiches will she eat in November?

5. The newest hand-held video-game craze is Spinning Space Mission. Using the spin button, you spin the space-mission spinner. If you get a 1, you travel 1,000 miles into space with 5 emergency force fuel points. A 2 sends you flying 2,000 miles into space with 10 force fuel points. How many force fuel points would you get if you spin a 9?

Make a Table or Chart

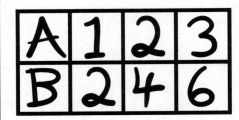

MAKE A TABLE OR CHART

Here's another strategy that helps organize information and thus better answer the first question in the problem-solving process: "What do we know?" Tables or charts are a way to organize two groups of data to better see what the relationship between the two groups might be. It helps make patterns and functions that create patterns more apparent.

For example, if we know that one can of beans costs 5¢, 2 cans are 10¢, and 3 cans are 15¢, by creating a table with this information, students will be able to figure out how much 8 cans of beans would cost (40¢). The table organizes the quantity and the cost so it's easier to see the relationship. As students use tables and charts, caution them as to how far to extend the data. In the case of the problem above, all we need to know is how much 8 cans cost. It wouldn't make sense to extend the table to 10 cans because that would be adding extra work and more information than we need.

Answers

1. 24 geckos
2. 13 boxes
3. 16 elephants
4. $24
5. 27 times

SAMPLE PROBLEMS

1. Gerty Gecko's wild serve in the last round of the Gecko Beach Volleyball Tournament sent the ball to the very top of a 12-foot coconut tree. How many 6-inch geckos standing on top of each other head-to-toe will it take to reach the ball and knock it out of the tree?

2. Bucky Beaver, owner of the Gnaw-It-All Pencil Company, is preparing his orders for the new school year. He packs the pencils a dozen to a box. Mr. Bernard Beaver of the Clever Beaver Elementary School needs 150 pencils. How many boxes should he order?

3. Madame Paula Pachyderm teaches ballet at the Elegant Elephant Dance Academy. Madame Pachyderm ordered 64 pink ballet slippers for the dancers in the upcoming recital. How many elephants will be dancing ballet in the recital?

4. Dexter is earning and saving money to buy a pair of Amazing-See-Through-Anything Super Glasses. So far he has earned half of the money he needs by mowing lawns in his neighborhood. He has mowed 3 lawns and received $4 for each one. How much do the glasses cost?

5. Clumsy Clyde is the clumsiest bat in the acrobat circus. He has no problem flipping, but landing is another story. He does 6 flips and 3 landings in each show. If he does 9 shows this week, how many times will he need to land?

STRATEGY 6:
Use Logical Reasoning

Logical reasoning is an approach that organizes and analyzes information so that it ultimately leads to a conclusion. Ideas that help students think logically include using lists, pictures, tables, charts, and looking for patterns. A logic matrix and Venn diagram are also helpful tools in organizing information in a logical way and seeing possibilities.

A logic matrix can help us organize facts and use the process of elimination to arrive at an answer. For example, "Jim lives in a blue house and drinks milk. Bert does not live in a green house. The person in the white house drinks juice. Joan drinks water. Where does Bert live?"

Person	House	Drink
Bert		Juice
Joan	Green	Water
Jim	Blue	Milk

Venn diagrams are also very useful for organizing information and supporting logical reasoning. For example, "The Eatalotsky family hosted Thanksgiving. There was a choice of main courses: turkey, ham, or both. Seven of the family members had turkey. Seven had ham. Since there are ten Eatalotskys, how many had both ham and turkey?" The Venn diagram helps provide an answer.

Answers

1. Webber, Fang, Leggs, and Spinner

2. 36

3. 1 member

4. Brando has a leopard, Andro has a gorilla, Alexo has an alligator, and Quentin has an octopus.

5. 11 inches

SAMPLE PROBLEMS

1. Arnold Arachnid is the biggest fan of the sensational singing spider group, The Rockin' Tarantulas. However, Arnold can never remember which spider is which. When looking at the stage, Spinner stands on the right side of the group and is farthest from Webber. Fang stands between Leggs and Webber. How are the spiders arranged on stage from left to right?

2. Sam Snoops, dog detective, could not remember the last number in the combination of his secret crime-fighting safe. He does remember that the number is higher than 30 but less than 40. It is an even number and the number in the ones column is double the number in the tens column. What is the last number in the combination?

3. There were 5 members of the Loopy Library Reading Club. There were only two books: *Ham Is Nice* and *Tails of a Dog*. 3 members read *Ham Is Nice*. 3 members read *Tails of a Dog*. How many members of the club read both books?

4. Brando, Andro, Alexo, and Quentin were sharing stories about their pet gorilla, alligator, leopard, and octopus. Quentin built a pool in his backyard for his pet. Brando had to run at lightning speed to keep up with his pet. Andro said it was difficult to take his pet for a walk in the woods because it always climbed trees. Alexo complained that people confused her pet with a crocodile. Who had which pet?

5. Felicia Frog was very proud of her long and sticky tongue. She bragged that it was 3 inches longer than her brother Felix's tongue. But Felix likes to remind her that their cousin Frankie's tongue is even 3 inches longer than hers. If Felix's tongue is 5 inches long, how long is Frankie's tongue?

Work Backward

WORK BACKWARD

Working backward is a good strategy to employ when we know how a problem ends up, but we don't know how it started. For example, if I went to the store and bought a hammer for $2.50 and the clerk gave me $2.50 change, how much money did I give the clerk to begin with? It is still a matter of applying the Five-Step Process and organizing information first, but the trick here is to know where to begin and to think about using inverse operations.

These types of problems are a great opportunity to help students see the usefulness of using letters or symbols to represent unknown quantities. For example, with the hammer problem we could think:

> *I gave the clerk x. And since I got back*
> *$2.50 and the hammer costs $2.50, then*
> *$2.50 + $2.50 = x.*
> x = $5.00

Answers

1. Larry leaves at 8:07 A.M.
   Louie leaves at 8:32 A.M.

2. $5

3. $138

4. $1.25

5. 920 pages

SAMPLE PROBLEMS

1. Lazy Larry Lizard and Lightning Louie Lizard are brothers. Larry does everything slowly and Louie does everything fast. The brothers arrive at school at 8:50 A.M. each morning. It takes Larry 43 minutes to get to school. It takes Louie 18 minutes to get to school. What time does each brother leave?

2. Shirley Squirrel had no time to collect her own acorns for the winter so she went to the Quickie Nut and Acorn Shop and bought 35 large acorns for 5¢ each. After paying for the acorns, Shirley received $3.25 in change. How much money did Shirley give the clerk?

3. Laurie Licorice just received her first paycheck from the There's Nothing Like Sugar candy store. She put half of the money in the bank. She used one-third of the other half to buy food, one-third was spent at Dollar Mart, and with the last $23.00 she bought a ticket to ride the all-day rocket coaster. How much money did Laurie earn in her first paycheck?

4. The Fancy Fly Catcher sells clothes for the well-dressed frog. Felicia Frog bought a fuzzy scarf for each of her 5 children. She paid $6.25 for the scarves. How much did each scarf cost?

5. Walter took his new book, *The New Adventures of Wilfred Wizard*, with him everywhere for a week. On Monday he read 100 pages. On Tuesday he read 120 pages. On Wednesday he read twice as many pages as he did on Tuesday. When he finished on Wednesday he was exactly halfway through the book. How many pages are in the book?

The Happy Hundred Word Problems 100

The "Happy Hundred Word Problems" are organized by the NCTM content standards. Within each standard section, problems are further organized and labeled by the major math concepts typically found in second-grade math curriculums. For example, Number and Operations is a large standard that includes concepts like place value, money, addition, and subtraction. There are specific word problems here for each of these concepts. The concept focus is marked in the upper left-hand corner of each problem. The answers are provided in the answer key on pp. 77–79.

As you introduce a problem, remind students to use the Five-Step Process. Keep the graphic organizer prominently displayed on a poster or chart, or give students a copy of their own to refer to. On each page you will find two problems with space for students to show their thinking. Encourage students to write down their solution process including any words, numbers, pictures, diagrams, or tables they use. This helps students with their thinking and understanding of the problem, while giving you more assessment information.

When assessing students' work on word problems, two major aspects need consideration: process and product. Observe students as they work on or discuss problems. Focus on what they say, and whether they use manipulatives, pictures, computation on scrap paper, or other strategies. When looking at their written products consider what skills they are exhibiting as well as what errors or misunderstandings they may be showing. This is why it is essential that students "show their thinking" as they solve a problem and explain their rationale.

Finally, have fun! These problems are designed to appeal to kids' sense of humor. Enjoy the situations and the process. Using what they know to solve word problems gives students a sense of mastery, accomplishment, meaning, and math power!

NUMBER AND OPERATIONS
PLACE VALUE, NUMBER, AND MONEY

1 Place Value With Tens and Ones

Cousin Snail went to the carnival.
She paid $5 to find out what her lucky
number was. The carnival lady told her,
"Your lucky number is 5 less than 5 tens
and 2 ones." What is Cousin Snail's
lucky number?

2 Place Value With Tens and Ones

Tomatotons have invaded the Earth. They
speak an unusual language. Instead of saying,
ten, they say, *pom*. Instead of saying, *one*,
they say, *pim*. Their leader said that if you can
guess the secret number, Earth will be saved!
He said the number is "pom, pom, pom, pom,
pom, pom, pom, pim, pim." What is the
secret number?

Place Value Through Hundreds

Brainix needed one more number to crack the code and find where his brother, Brawnix, hid his lucky socks. Brainix had some clues. The number had 3 digits. There was an odd number in the hundreds place. There was a zero in the tens place. The 3 digits added up to 9. The number was less than 800, but more than 700. What was it?

Place Value Through Hundreds

Smanx is manager of his school's whistleball team. He has 3 number stencils to use to put numbers on the backs of the team shirts. His stencils are for numbers 2, 5, and 9. Players can wear 1-, 2-, or 3-digit numbers on their backs, but no digits can be repeated on a shirt. How many shirts can Smanx number? What would the players' numbers be?

Skip Counting

Mizingos are strange creatures. They have 2 heads, 5 legs, 6 arms, and 3 ears. If there were 5 mizingos in your front yard, how many legs would you see?

6 **Skip Counting**

Dr. Why is trying to solve a mystery. He must find one more number to open the secret vault that holds the Ancient Secret of the Lost Peanut Butter. He knows the first five numbers of the combination are 16–20–24–28–32. What do you think is the final number? Why?

7   **Skip Counting**

The Mr. Snowy Ice Cream truck is driving down Dogface Drive. The truck is at #18. As it drives by the next 6 houses on the same side of the street, the numbers keep getting higher. The truck finally stops at the 7th house. What is the address?

8   **Skip Counting**

Professor Pattern knew something was wrong. The numbers he found scattered on the carpet were 12, 6, 15, 9, 18, 3, 21, 4, and 24, but they were supposed to form a pattern. They were not in any order he could see and it appeared that one number did not belong with the group. What is the proper order and which number does not belong?

9 — Ordinal Numbers

The new Howhiareya Apartment Building opened recently. It is 32 floors high. Max lives on the 5th floor. Smax lives 8 floors above him and Fax lives 9 floors above Smax. How many floors must Max go up to visit Fax?

10 — More or Fewer

Wazgood Bookatoosky is best friends with Izgood Bowlathreesky. They played a game where every vowel in your name is worth 2 points and every consonant is worth 1 point. Whose name is worth the most?

11 **Rounding to the Nearest Ten**

In the caterpillar-chasing contest, 40 points gets you a blue ribbon, 30 points gets you a red ribbon, and 20 points gets you a yellow ribbon. If your score is between these numbers, whichever level you are closest to is the ribbon you get. Zig scored 28 points. Zag scored 36 points. Zog scored 31 points. What ribbons should they each get?

12 **Money**

Snacko wants to buy chocolate-covered cheese balls from the vending machine. They cost 30¢. He has only nickels and dimes. How many different ways can he pay for the cheese balls? List the different ways.

Math Word Problems Made Easy: Grade 2 Scholastic Teaching Resources

13 Money

Professor Stinkbug is planning to buy a new magnifying glass to better observe his insect friends. Magnifying glasses are on sale for 72¢ each. How can he pay using the fewest number of coins?

14 Money

Cranky, Frankie, and Spanky went to the bank(y). They wanted to exchange their coins for dollar bills. Cranky gave the teller 2 half-dollars, 1 quarter, and 2 dimes. Frankie handed over 3 quarters, 2 dimes, and a nickel. Spanky handed in 5 dimes, 4 nickels, and 5 pennies. Who got exactly a $1 bill from the teller?

15   **Money: Making Change**

Pez went to Yammy's yard sale. He bought a shoelace for 7¢ and a yo-yo string for 15¢. He paid with 3 dimes. How much change should he get back?

16   **Money: Making Change**

The Chicken That Played First Base

Tina brought her cousin, Tiny, to see the new hit movie, *The Chicken That Played First Base*. The tickets were 15¢ each. Tina paid and was given a dime in change. How much money did she give the clerk?

17 | Single-Digit Addition

The buses were ready to leave for the Goof-Off Games. Four teams were going: Waxonville, Jaxonville, Paxonville, and Snortly. Waxonville has 7 players. Jaxonville has 9, Paxonville 6, and Snortly 5. The A Bus has 15 seats. The B Bus has 12 seats. Which teams should ride on the A bus? Which teams should ride on the B bus?

18 | Single-Digit Addition

John bought a dozen Giganto raisins. Giganto raisins are sold in "snack packs" with 5 in a pack, "munch bags" with 4 in a bag, or "yum boxes" with 7 in a box. John bought 2 different containers to get his dozen raisins. What were they?

19   Single-Digit Addition

Roscoe is spinning the Lucky Eight Double Wheel of Chance at the carnival. On each wheel are the numbers 0 to 8. Both wheels are spun at the same time. If the numbers on the two wheels add up to 8, Roscoe wins. How many different ways can Roscoe win?

20   Single-Digit Addition

Petunia was playing Toe Throw against Marigold and Daisy. Each girl scored the same number of points in the first round. In the second round, Daisy scored 7 points. Marigold had a total score of 13 points after two rounds. Petunia scored 1 more point than Daisy in round 2 and finished with 12 points. Who won the Toe Throw match?

21 Single-Digit Addition

Mrs. Mango was ordering books for her class library. She bought 3 copies of *Tales of a Turkey*, 5 copies of *The Chicken's Revenge*, 6 copies of *Squid Stories*, and 1 copy of *The Encyclopedia of Eagles and Egrets*. She already had 7 books in the Feathered Friends section of her library. If she adds the new books that belong in that section, how many Feathered Friends books will she have?

22 Single-Digit Addition: Three or More Addends

Peabody was playing a new game, Toss Your Boss. He threw his boss, Mr. Meany, four times. Mr. Meany landed on the 5 space twice. He landed on the 8 space once and on the 3 space one time. How many points did Peabody score before Mr. Meany fired him?

23

**Single-Digit Addition
and Subtraction**

Rizrox is putting his Lunar Collector Cards in his album. His last page has space for 13 cards. He has 9 on the page now. His pal, Zipzag, gives him 5 more cards. How many cards will not fit on the page?

24

Single-Digit Subtraction

Gazookians and Bazookians have landed on Earth. 3 Gazookians and 4 Bazookians were spotted at the mall. Gazookians have 3 legs. Bazookians have 2 legs. Were there more Bazookian legs or Gazookian legs at the mall? How many more?

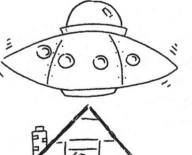

25   Single-Digit Subtraction

"We must bring the electrical current point rating down to 7 exactly," said Spaceship Commander Zog.

Ensign Eggo said, "It's at 14 now, sir." Turning off the scrambler will lower the point rating 5 points. Turning off the radio will lower it 3 points. Turning off the refrigerator will lower it 2 points. What should Commander Zog do? Why?

26   Single-Digit Subtraction

Artie Objeck was making one of his famous "glue-on" paintings. This one was called "Shoe for You." He glued on 8 blue shoes, 3 black shoes, and 6 yellow shoes. When he hung it up there were only 7 pairs of shoes on it. Artie had borrowed some of his mother's shoes and she wanted them back. How many shoes did she take back?

27 Single-Digit Addition and Subtraction

The Circus Triplets all have their birthdays on the same day, June 14th. Jumping Jack is 9 years old. Juggling Jake is 2 years older than Geronimo Gina. Gina is 5 years younger than Jack. How old is Jake?

28 Single-Digit Addition and Subtraction

In the game of Numero, players wear specially numbered shirts. To score, two players must hold hands and cross the finish line together. If the numbers on their shirts add up to an odd number they score a point. Bingo is wearing #11. Boppo is wearing #3. Beppo is wearing #4 and Bippo is wearing #12. What combinations of players could score a point?

29   **Missing Addends**

Zeke collects bottle caps.
He has 12 Penguin Pop caps,
5 Rat's Root Beer, 2 Gorilla
Grape, and the rest are
Kookie Kola caps. He has 24
caps in his collection. How
many are Kookie Kola caps?

30   **Missing Addends**

Bella said, "Oh, no. The piece of paper
with Grandpa Greatknuckle's phone
number got ripped. All I can read is
'215-34_ _.' The last two numbers were
ripped off. I remember the whole thing
adds up to 16 and the last two digits
were lower than 2 and not the same."
What are the last two numbers?

31 Three or More Addends

Zagwort was traveling across the galaxy. He left Planet Weezil and flew 7 miles to Gazmo. He rested there for 3 days, then flew 5 more miles to Zigzag. He rested for 2 more days and then flew 6 miles to Flipflop. How many miles is it from Weezil to Flipflop?

32 Three or More Addends

Uncle Sinker went out fishing for 4 days. He caught 8 rare bugnose bass on the first day, 2 tuner fish on the second day, 9 fuzz fish on the third day, and another tuner fish on the last day. How many fish did he catch?

33   Addition Rules Pattern

Casper is selling his very popular homemade potato shoes. He sold his first pair for $7. The second pair he sold for $10. The third pair he sold for $13. If the pattern continues, for how much will he sell the 5th pair?

34   Subtraction Rules Pattern

John went into The Shrinker weighing 14 pounds. He came out weighing 7 pounds. Jim went in weighing 15 pounds and came out weighing 8 pounds. Tiny went in weighing 8 pounds and came out weighing a pound. What was the dial on the shrinker set to do?

Double-Digit Addition and Subtraction

The Big Bug Basketball Championship was played between the Trenton Termites and the New York Gnats. The Gnats won by 11 points. The Termites scored 2 points less than their old record of 60 points. What was the final score?

Double-Digit Addition Without Regrouping

"Play the game, score 60 points, and win a stuffed cockroach doll!" yelled the manager of the Toss-the-Noodle-on-the-Onion game. Pinky and Stinky decided they would try the game. They agreed to put their points together and share the cockroach doll. Pinky took 4 turns and scored 11 points on each turn. Stinky took 3 turns and scored 6 points on the first 2 turns, and 2 points on her last turn. The girls put their points together. Do they need more points to win? If so, how many more?

37

Double-Digit Addition Without Regrouping

It takes Rufus an hour to go 10 miles in his Slowmobile. It's 22 miles from Bingo to Bango. It's 21 miles from Bango to Bongo. It's 23 miles from Bongo to Bungo. How far is it from Bungo to Bingo?

38

Double-Digit Addition Without Regrouping

Diane scored 27 points playing tuna hockey. Dion scored 32 points. Delon scored 63 points. Dilby scored 1 point less than Delon. Darby scored 64 points. Two of these players scored a total of 95 points together. Which two?

39

**Double-Digit Addition
With Regrouping**

Snow was falling fast on the
town of Tundra. 13 inches
of snow fell the first
night. Twice as
much fell on the
second night. The
third night, only a
foot fell. How much
snow fell on Tundra?

40

**Double-Digit Addition
With Regrouping**

The target Scut painted on his little
brother, Scoot, had scoring rings
with 13, 14, 15, 16, 18, and 20
written on them. Scut threw 2
mudballs and scored a total of 32
points before Scoot scooted away
to tell his mother. Which 2 rings did
Scut hit?

41   Double-Digit Addition With Regrouping

Freaky Fries are sold in three sizes: a small costs 23¢, a medium is 41¢, and a large is 62¢. Tango has 14¢ and Mango has 27¢. They want to buy some fries and split them. Which size should they buy? Will they get change? If so, how much?

42   Double-Digit Addition Regrouping With Three Addends

Spunky has a shelf in his room to hold his trophies. He's got a bowling trophy that weighs 15 pounds, a golf trophy that weighs 21 pounds, and a 17-pound trophy for brushing his teeth really well. He just got a new 18-pound trophy for sock washing. The shelf can hold 60 pounds. Can he safely put his new trophy on the shelf? Why or why not?

43 — Double-Digit Addition Regrouping With Three Addends

Professor Prune is testing his new invention, the Raisinator. The Raisinator measures the amount of raisins in a person's house. He checked 3 rooms each day. It showed readings of 34, 37, and 28 on Tuesday at his house. Readings were 36, 38, and 29 on Wednesday. Which day had fewer raisins?

44 — Adding Three-Digit Numbers Without Regrouping

Famous artist, I.M. Mesee is having a show of his 129 most famous paintings. On Friday night 124 people came. On Saturday 163 people came. On Monday 110 people came. How many people saw the show on Friday and Saturday?

Math Word Problems Made Easy: Grade 2 Scholastic Teaching Resources

45

Adding Three-Digit Numbers Without Regrouping

Goodella is reading the new *Willy Wonder* book. It has 888 pages. She read the first 122 pages on Monday. If she does the same thing for 2 more days, how many pages will she have read?

46

Adding Three-Digit Numbers With Regrouping

Mrs. Yelltoomuch had her class make paper hats. They made 329 hats. Mrs. Iyelltoo's class wanted to do this also. They made 536 hats. Mr. Loudlee's class did not want to be left out so they made 418 hats. Two classes put their hats together and had a total of 747 hats. Which two classes did this?

47 — Adding Three-Digit Numbers With Regrouping

Oscar loves Grandma Mitzy's fish-eye soup. Oscar visited her 126 days last year. This year he spent 158 days visiting her. Every day he's with her he eats a bowl of her soup. How many bowls of soup has he eaten in the last two years?

48 — Double-Digit Subtraction Without Regrouping

The three-toed Teraxus weighs 64 pounds. The Refrigeratus weighs 58 pounds. Bill weighs 42 pounds. Which animal weighs 16 pounds more than Bill?

Math Word Problems Made Easy: Grade 2 • Scholastic Teaching Resources

49

Double-Digit Subtraction Without Regrouping

Kooky Cooking Contest

Swarma scored 329 points in the Kooky Cooking Contest for her Upside-Down Garbage-Can Cake. Her sister, Parma scored 112 points for her Toothpaste Surprise Pie. How many more points did Swarma score than Parma?

50

Double-Digit Subtraction Without Regrouping

Ernie has to reach Waldo City by 9:00 P.M. The trip is 340 miles. He leaves Acorn Junction at 4:30 P.M. He drives 120 miles to Peachy and arrives at 6:15 P.M. How much farther does he have to go?

51 Double-Digit Subtraction With Regrouping

"I can give you 68 lint balls for your collection if you give me a penny for each one," Herman told Hazel.

"I'll take them! Then I'll have a total of 99!" Hazel replied.

How many lint balls did Hazel have to start with?

52 Double-Digit Subtraction With Regrouping

John, Jim, and Junior all started the marble contest with 40 marbles each. At the end of the contest, Jim had 17, Joe had 16, and Junior had 14. Who lost 26 of their marbles?

Math Word Problems Made Easy: Grade 2   Scholastic Teaching Resources

53 Double-Digit Subtraction With Regrouping

The Smelly brothers went on vacation to Rancho Stinko. They spent a lot of their money on souvenir dirty socks. Smedley had $50 and spent $22. Smiley had $42 and spent $17. Smitty had $36 and spent $9. Who has less than $30 left?

54 Three-Digit Subtraction Without Regrouping

The Loco Express was heading for Blue Buzzard Gulch. There were 944 passengers on board. 316 got off in Cactus Creek and 428 got off in Kickamee Canyon. How many passengers are left on the train?

55   Three-Digit Subtraction Without Regrouping

Jaxon saw there were 488 looneypops in the prize box on Mr. Jam's desk. 225 were blue or yellow. A dozen were red. The rest were orange. How many were orange?

56   Three-Digit Subtraction With Regrouping

Dastardly Dan got detention for 152 days after he glued Mrs. Yacky's shoes to the floor. He has been in detention for 10 weeks now (7 days a week). How many days of detention does he have left?

57 **Three-Digit Subtraction With Regrouping**

Stubborn Stan was drawing with a marker on the windows. "If you keep this up, I'll take $1.25 from your allowance for every minute it continues," said Mom. Stan kept it up for 5 minutes. His allowance is $8.70. How much did he have left?

58 **Multiplication**

Mysterious Melissa tried to stump her brainy brother Boris. She said, "I'm thinking of a number that is odd. It is between 10 and 30. It is more than 3 x 5."

Boris asked, "Is it less than 3 x 6?"

"Yes," replied Melissa.

What was Melissa's number?

Multiplication

The Yinx is an unusual bird. It flies 5 miles a day, but it only flies on days that begin with the letter "T." How far does the Yinx fly in 2 weeks?

Multiplication

Wayne eats 3 bowls of Turkey-Flavored Yummie-O's at breakfast. He does this for 3 days. Wanda eats 2 bowls of Yummie-O's a day. She does this for 5 days. Who eats the most Yummie-O's?

61 Division

Pez is a nice guy. When he got a dozen chocolate-covered squid as a birthday present, he was ready to share them equally with his brothers, Piz and Poz. How many chocolate-covered squid should each brother get?

62 Division

Renaldo made a super pepperoni-and-sour-cream sandwich for his cooking-class graduation party. It is 4 feet long. He cut it into 14 pieces. If each person gets 2 pieces, how many people can Renaldo serve?

Unit Fractions

The cream-filled pickle cake at Al's birthday party was huge. Mars got 4 pieces. Al got 2 pieces. Slim got 1 piece and Jim got 1 piece. All the pieces are gone. Who got $\frac{1}{4}$ of the cake?

Unit Fractions

Harry had been hungry all night. He ate $\frac{1}{10}$ of the KooKoo CoCo Candy Bar at 7:00 P.M. He ate $\frac{3}{10}$ at 8:00 P.M. He ate $\frac{3}{10}$ more at 8:30 P.M. It is now 9:00 P.M. How much of the candy bar is left?

Math Word Problems Made Easy: Grade 2   Scholastic Teaching Resources

65   Unit Fractions

John put $\frac{1}{6}$ of the class dirt pile in his pockets. Jay took $\frac{3}{6}$ of it. Jung took some too. There is $\frac{1}{6}$ left. How much of the dirt pile did Jung take?

66   Fraction of a Set

Foodella is on an odd diet. She only eats foods that start with the letter "O" on days that start with the letter "T." She eats foods that start with the letter "G" on days that start with "S." What fraction of the week can Foodella eat oatmeal?

67   Fraction of a Number

Pirate Peanut dug up some buried treasure. He found 12 coins. $\frac{1}{4}$ of the coins he found had Long John Nasty's picture on them. The rest had a fuzzy bunny on them. How many coins had fuzzy bunnies on them?

68   Length: Feet and Inches

Twelve-year-old Pandora told her brothers, "I'm 14 inches taller than you, Rodney, and 6 inches taller than you, Roscoe." Rodney is 4 feet tall and 10 years old. How tall is Pandora?

69 — Length: Feet and Yards

Ronzoni was at the bottom of Kooky Canyon. Kooky Canyon is 7 yards* deep. His brother, Tonzoni, was looking for a rope to throw to Ron to get him out of the canyon. He found one rope that was 20 feet, 6 inches long and another rope that was 18 feet, 36 inches long. Which rope should he use?

* 1 yard = 3 feet; 1 foot = 12 inches

70 — Length: Centimeters and Meters

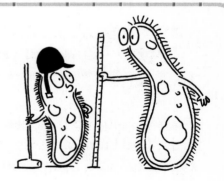

To play on the Minuscule Microbes Polo Team you must be at least 1 meter* tall. Peanut Paramecium wants to join the team. He was measured at the tryouts and found to be 90 centimeters tall. How much taller must he be before he can play on the team?

* 1 meter = 100 centimeters

71 Weight: Pounds

Larry the lifeguard hurt his arm. His doctor warned him that he should not carry anything weighing more than a pound or less than a pound. His mom asked him to help carry her shopping bags into the house. The blue bag had 4 bags of popcorn in it. The red one had a watermelon. The yellow one had a loaf of bread. Which bag should Larry probably carry?

72 Weight: Pounds and Ounces

Disco is going to mail his pet turtle, Old Lumpy, to Florida for a vacation. Old Lumpy weighs 32 ounces*. It costs $1 a pound to mail turtles. How much will it cost to mail Old Lumpy?

* 16 ounces = 1 pound

Math Word Problems Made Easy: Grade 2   Scholastic Teaching Resources

73 Weight: Kilograms

Glinda found 3 bars of gold at the bottom of the old mine shaft. One was marked "2 pounds." One was marked "2 kilograms*." The last was marked "4 pounds." The elevator in the mine can hold only 84 pounds. Glinda weighs 70 pounds. She can make only one trip up from the mine. Which bar of gold should she bring on the elevator with her? Why?

* 1 kilogram = 2.2 pounds

74 Capacity: Customary Units

Count Drinkula must drink 1 pint* of his favorite beverage, tomato juice, before the sun rises. So far he has had 1 cup of tomato juice. The sun will rise in 1 hour. How much more does he need to drink?

* 1 pint = 2 cups

75   Capacity: Customary Units

In the Second Annual One-Horned Cow Milking Contest, Billy Bob got 5 pints* of milk, Billy Joe got 1 quart, and Bobby Bill got 8 cups. Who got the most milk?

* 1 pint = 2 cups; 1 quart = 2 pints

76   Capacity: Customary Units

The Toastox is an animal that drinks 10 liters of water a day. The zoo keeper has a tea kettle, a gallon jug, and a fish tank to put the water in. Which should she fill with the Toastox's water?

Math Word Problems Made Easy: Grade 2   Scholastic Teaching Resources

77 — Temperature: Fahrenheit

Careful Calvin is going outside to skateboard at 4:00 P.M. He is wearing shorts, a T-shirt, sneakers, helmet, and pads. Is the temperature most likely 32°F, 48°F, or 75°F?

78 — Temperature: Celsius

Hot-Headed Hannah wants to practice her ice-skating routine on the pond for the Ant Olympics. She sees the forecast for Monday is 30°C. For Tuesday it's 0°C, and for Wednesday it's 10°C. Which day should she go skating on the pond? Why?

79 **Time**

On Doogie's digital clock, the digits are adding up to 10. It is not 4:20 yet, but it's after 4:09. What time is it on his clock?

80 **Time**

It is now 20 minutes before 4:00 A.M. In half an hour Joe the vampire will go to the dentist. He will be there for 1 hour having his teeth whitened. Then he will walk 10 minutes home to his castle. What time will Joe get home?

81   Time

Canyu lives in Slippery City. He needs to be in Toastville at 3:00 P.M. for a slipper-repair appointment. He found a bus schedule, but the bottom was ripped off. The top of the schedule shows buses leave every hour starting at 10:00 A.M. The 10:00 A.M. bus arrives in Toastville at 1:00 P.M. What bus should Canyu take to get to Toastville on time?

82   Time/Calendar

Pengy's birthday is on June 28th. Pongo wants to order Pengy a new pair of flippers. The Floppy Flipper Company guarantees delivery by truck in 10 days for a price of $10. You can also order delivery by plane. This takes 3 days and costs $20. The company does not deliver on weekends. It is Tuesday, June 17th. Pongo wants to make sure Pengy gets his present on time, but doesn't want to spend more money than he has to. What should he do?

83   Time to 10 Minutes

The space bus to Planet Bizbo leaves at 2:30 P.M. Gazma wants to be there on time. It takes 40 minutes to walk to the bus from her house. It is now 10:00 A.M. What's the latest she should leave her house?

84   Elapsed Time

Lefty Luna Lava is getting ready for her big Toadball game tonight. She gets up at 6:00 A.M. and drinks 2 glasses of asparagus juice. She runs 1 mile backwards for one hour. Then she does her stretches for half an hour. Now she is ready for practice. Practice takes an hour. What time will practice be over?

Bar Graph

The Loonyville School lunchroom was setting up their menu. They did a survey to see which sandwiches the children wanted most. This is a graph of the results. Which was the second-favorite choice? How many more votes did the favorite sandwich get?

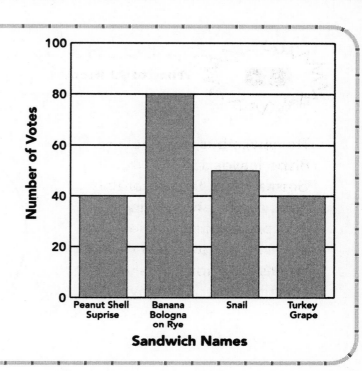

86 **Pictograph**

Channel Z wants to know which shows its viewers like best. This pictograph shows the results of their research. How many viewers liked the least favorite show?

Channel Z Viewers' Favorite TV Shows

Show	Votes
Spooky Sid Presents	🦇🦇🦇🦇
Fangs A Lot	🦇🦇🦇
Full Moon Fun	🦇🦇
Cooking With Creature	🦇🦇🦇🦇🦇

🦇 = 5 viewers

DATA ANALYSIS AND PROBABILITY

87 Venn Diagram

Two new sports were recently added to the Forest Animal Olympics. Here's a diagram showing who competed in the new events. How many animals participated in the Nut-Gathering Relay?

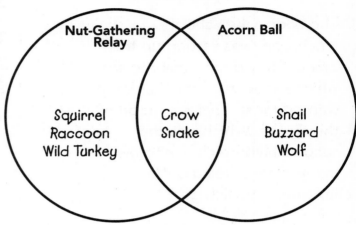

Forest Animal Olympics Participants

Nut-Gathering Relay

Acorn Ball

Squirrel
Raccoon
Wild Turkey

Crow
Snake

Snail
Buzzard
Wolf

88 Probability

Slimy Steve's Surprise Bag had 2 toad tongues, 10 newt noses, 11 salamanders, and 10 turkey toes in it. What would you most likely pick out of the bag?

89   **Predicting Outcomes**

Rascally Roscoe set up his Spinner of Chance at the
Fair. It is divided evenly into 10 sections. There is a
number in each section. The numbers are 11, 7, 3,
1, 55, 69, 29, 8, 35, and 19. Use these words to
describe the probability of the spinner landing on
certain numbers: *likely, unlikely, certain, impossible.*

    a. a number below 70
    b. an odd number
    c. a number that is above 80
    d. an even number

90   **Solid Shapes**

Marilyn Martian was stuck on Earth.
She wanted to make a vehicle that
would help her get quickly to the
emergency launch site. She found a
cart and a set of molds that she could
use to make solids. Which solids
might help her move the cart along—
cubes, pyramids, cylinders, spheres,
or rectangular prisms? Why?

91   Solid Shapes: Faces, Corners, Edges

On the *Guess My Shape?* TV show, the first guest said, "I have 6 faces, 8 corners, and 12 edges."

The second guest said, "I have 5 faces, 5 corners, and 8 edges."

The third guest said, "I have 2 faces, 0 corners, and 0 edges."

Which guest was the pyramid?

92   Solid and Plane Figures

Quincy opened up the Build-Your-Own-Solid kit. Inside he found 2 squares the same size and 4 rectangles all the same size. What solid shape could he build?

93 Shapes: Sides and Corners

Hester had two trapezoid-shaped tables. She put them together so she and her friends could play their favorite card game, "Go Wish." The new table had 6 sides and 6 corners. What shape was it?

94 Symmetry

Alfreda Alphabet put three letters on the table. She said, "One of these little beauties is symmetrical." The letters were all capitals. One was the 7th letter of the alphabet, one was the 10th, and the last was the 15th. What was the symmetrical letter?

95 Perimeter

Biff is building a pen for his new rare pet, Fuzzy the fire-breathing hamster. Fuzzy's pen has to be square. Biff measured how long he wants the first side. He wants it to be 5 feet long. What will the perimeter of the pen be?

96 Perimeter

The New Center for the Exploration of Silliness has a perimeter of 32 feet. The south wall is 8 feet across. The east wall and west wall are each 8 feet across. How wide is the north wall?

97   Area

Peninsula has invented a new game—Banana Ball. There will be 5 players on each side. She is drawing the lines for the court on the blacktop with chalk. It is a rectangle with a length of 10 feet and a width of 6 feet. What will the area of the court be?

98   Area

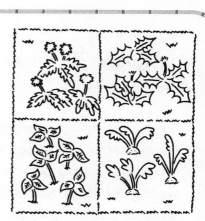

The Ghastleys' garden is unusual. It has a perimeter of 16 yards. Each side is equal. The garden is divided into fourths. $\frac{1}{4}$ is weeds, $\frac{1}{4}$ is thistles, $\frac{1}{4}$ is poison ivy, and $\frac{1}{4}$ is turnips. What is the area of the turnips?

99   Perimeter and Area

Thor wants to write his name on his lawn in the backyard so it will be visible to planes and helicopters that pass over. He is cutting the letters out of the grass with his lawn mower. The area of the letter "T" is 5 square yards. What is the perimeter?

100   Volume

Nero was using cubes to build a tower. His tower was 5 cubes wide, 2 cubes long, and 5 cubes high. His brother Caesar built a tower that was 4 cubes wide, 3 cubes long, and 5 cubes high. Which tower had the greater volume?

ANSWER KEY

Number and Operations

Place Value, Number, and Money

1. 47

2. 72

3. 702

4. 15 shirts: 2, 5, 9, 25, 29, 52, 59, 92, 95, 259, 295, 529, 592, 925, 952

5. 25 legs

6. 36. There is a pattern of counting by fours.

7. #32 Dogface Drive

8. 3, 6, 9, 12, 15, 18, 21, 24 (or reverse); 4 does not belong.

9. 17 floors

10. They are both worth 26 points.

11. Zig–red ribbon
Zag–blue ribbon
Zog–red ribbon

12. 4 ways:
6 nickels OR 4 nickels and 1 dime
OR 2 nickels and 2 dimes OR
3 dimes

13. 1 half-dollar, 2 dimes, 2 pennies

14. Frankie

15. 8¢

16. 40¢

Addition and Subtraction

17. Bus A–Jaxonville and Paxonville;
Bus B–Waxonville and Snortly

18. 1 "yum box" and 1 "snack pack"

19. 9 ways: 0+8, 8+0, 1+7, 7+1, 2+6, 6+2, 5+3, 3+5, 4+4

20. Marigold with 13 points

21. 16 books

22. 21 points

23. 1 card

24. Gazookians; 1 more leg

25. Turn off the refrigerator and the scrambler, because 5+2=7 and 14–7=7.

26. 3 shoes

27. 6 years old

28. Boppo and Bippo; Bingo and Bippo; Beppo and Bingo; and Boppo and Beppo

29. 5 Kookie Kola caps

30. 0,1 or 1,0

31. 18 miles

32. 20 fish

33. $19

34. Subtract 7 pounds

35. Gnats–69, Termites–58

36. Yes; 2 more points

37. 66 miles

38. Delon and Dion

39. 51 inches

40. 14 and 18

ANSWER KEY

41. Medium fries; no change

42. No. The total weight of the trophies is 71 pounds—too heavy for the shelf.

43. Tuesday

44. 287 people

45. 366 pages

46. Mr. Loudlee's and Mrs. Yelltoomuch's classes

47. 284 bowls

48. The Refrigeratus

49. 217 points

50. 220 miles

51. 31 lint balls

52. Junior

53. All of them

54. 200 passengers

55. 251 looneypops

56. 82 days

57. $2.45

Multiplication and Division

58. 17

59. 20 miles

60. Wanda

61. 4 each

62. 7 people

Fractions

63. Al

64. 3/10

65. 1/6

66. 2/7

67. 9 coins

Measurement

68. 5 feet, 2 inches (or 62 inches)

69. 18 feet, 36 inches long

70. 10 centimeters

71. Yellow

72. $2

73. The bar marked 2 kilograms. It gives her the most gold, but still meets the elevator's weight limit.

74. 1 cup

75. Billy Bob

76. Fish tank

77. 75°F

78. On Tuesday, because the pond will be frozen.

79. 4:15

80. 5:20 A.M.

81. 12:00 P.M. bus

82. Order delivery by plane. Delivery by truck won't get the present there on time.

83. 1:50 P.M.

84. 8:30 A.M.

ANSWER KEY

Data Analysis and Probability

85. Snail; 30 votes

86. 10 viewers

87. 5 animals

88. A salamander

89. a. certain
b. likely
c. impossible
d. unlikely

Geometry

90. Cylinders and spheres because they can roll.

91. The second guest

92. Rectangular prism

93. Hexagon

94. O, the 15th letter

95. 20 feet

96. 8 feet

97. 60 square feet

98. 4 square yards

99. 12 yards

100. Caesar's tower. It had a volume of 60 cubes.

TEACHER'S NOTES

Math Word Problems Made Easy:
Grade 2